PLAY
WITH YOUR
PUMPKINS

PLAY
WITH YOUR
PUMPKINS

by **Joost Elffers** and **Saxton Freymann**

Text by **Johannes van Dam**

A Joost Elffers Book

Stewart, Tabori and Chang
New York

Edited by Alexandra Childs
Photography by John Fortunato, New York

Designed by Erik Thé, Amsterdam

Published in 1998 by **Joost Elffers Books**
Distributed in the U.S. by **Stewart, Tabori & Chang**,
a division of U.S. Media Holdings, Inc.
115 West 18th Street, New York 10011

Distributed in Canada by **General Publishing Company Ltd.**
30 Lesmill Road, Don Mills, Ontario, Canada M3B 2T6

Sold in Australia by **Peribo Pty Ltd.**
58 Beaumont Road, Mount Kuring-gai, NSW 2080, Australia

Distributed in all other territories by **Grantham Book Services Ltd.**
Isaac Newton Way, Alma Park Industrial Estate
Grantham, Lincolnshire, NG31 9SD, England

Library of Congress Cataloging-in-Publication Data:

Elffers, Joost
      Play with your pumpkins/ by Joost Elffers and Saxton Freymann
      Text by Johannes van Dam
      p.   cm.
      "A Joost Elffers book."
      ISBN: 1-55670-848-3
      1. Cookery (Pumpkin) 2. Pumpkin. I. Freymann, Saxton.
      II. Dam, Johannes van. III. Title.
      TX803.P93E44   1998   98-17155
      641.6'562-dc21   CIP

Printed in Germany by Druckerei Uhl
A Joost Elffers/Andreas Landshoff Production

10 9 8 7 6 5 4

Contents

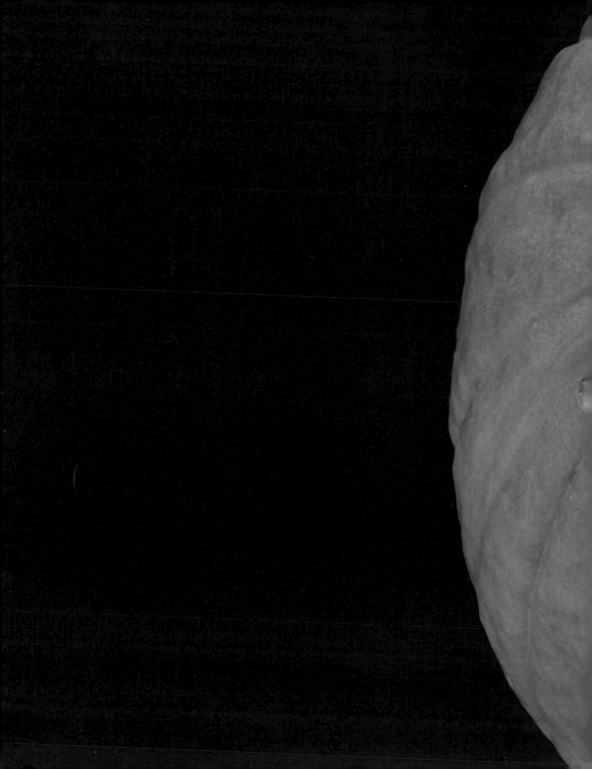

A Nose
for Design

HE pumpkin is more than an oversized vegetable or a jack-o'-lantern. It has, in fact, a very long history — once considered a symbol of the whole world, a container of everything ever created.

Early societies saw symbolism and spiritual significance in many natural objects, from rocks and trees to seeds and, yes, the pumpkin. Today much of that awe and magic is forgotten — except by children, who, in their innocence and unbridled imagination, *see* all kinds of suggestions and meaning (like ghosts and bogeymen) in even the most ordinary objects. It is the creative goal of this book to help keep that miraculous world alive.

Joost Elffers and Saxton Freymann are the team that brought together the concept and artwork that highlight the pages that follow. As the foreign-born contributor, Elffers was not encumbered by the traditional view of the pumpkin as a Halloween jack-o'-lantern with cookie-cutter features on its face.

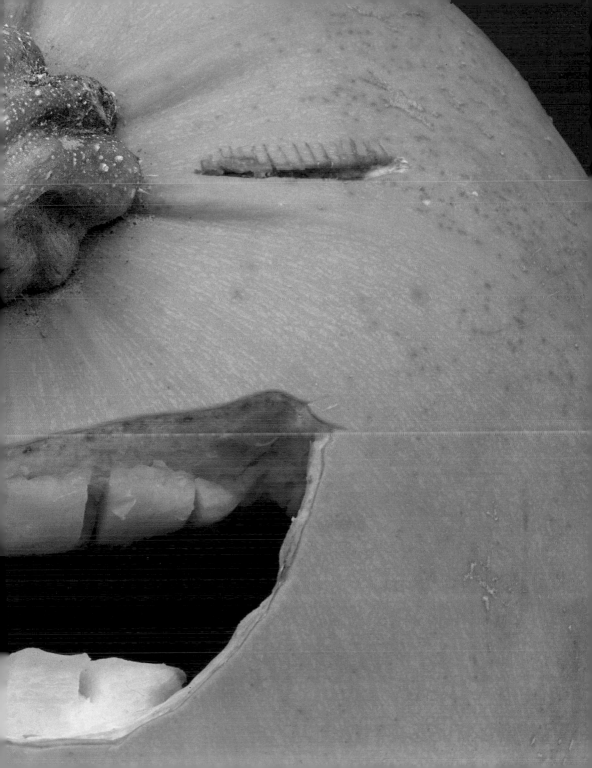

New York artist Freymann carved Elffers' vision into exciting human and animal features showing a stunning range of facial expressions and emotions.

"The pumpkin's stem is obviously a nose," says Elffers, "the natural starting point for creating a face." The "life lines" converging on the nose seem to dictate the mood of the created visage. Add to this Freymann's adroit, but always simple, carving out of mouth and eyes — and you have a magical transformation of a vegetable into a highly charged representation of living emotion.

In the Halloween tradition, the jack-o'-lantern's face is carved on the side of the pumpkin. Clearly, if the pumpkin is to be a lantern, the stem must be on top so that the pumpkin's bottom will provide a stable base. But it took a foreigner's perception — that is, an outsider's view — to see that "the American way of carving ignores the pumpkin's natural nose. This is surely a missed opportunity!" Not that Elffers wishes to replace the old tradition — but rather he'd like to add something new to it. He envisions that his and Freymann's creative way of carving a pumpkin-with-a-nose* will someday be an accepted part of Halloween history.

* The new age of carved pumpkins first surfaced in the popular *Play with Your Food*, published by Stewart, Tabori & Chang (1997). The book offers simple techniques for carving one's own fruit and vegetable creatures, with a special section on pumpkins.

In addition to being inspirational the pumpkin images in this book are meant to purely delight and amuse the reader. It is hoped that they will stimulate people to look at pumpkins in an entirely new and different way — the way that artists and designers (and sometimes foreigners!) look at many commonplace objects in their surroundings. They more readily see the suggestiveness of shapes and forms beyond their literal identity and function. "Why," they might ask, "must a pumpkin's face be carved on its side when there is such a natural nose begging to be the center of an incredibly expressive face?" Creative people embrace such opportunities to add more meaning — in this case, a fresh perception — to the ordinary things in their lives.

In these pages you will see what this kind of perception yields. And the process might very well reveal how to look not just at pumpkins, but at everything around you, through the magical eyes of a child.

Beyond the creative features, *Play with Your Pumpkins* offers twenty-four sweet and savory pumpkin recipes from around the world — not to mention an entertaining cultural history of this most remarkable vegetable.

The History of the Pumpkin

New-World Food or Whole World Food?

 IKE most of us, the pumpkin is a member of an extended family; some members don't even remotely resemble each other. This family is known as the *Cucurbitaceae* or cucurbits. Botanists consider it a small family, with "only" 650 species. Its members are commonly identified as climbing, trailing, or creeping herbaceous plants that grow very quickly. The fruits of these plants are all rather large and meaty in substance, and some of them are deliciously edible. While it may be common knowledge to some, others might be surprised to learn that the cucumber is an important member of this family. The gherkin and the melon are also close relatives, as are the zucchini or *courgette*, the marrow, the watermelon, the gourd, and the chayote.

There are the more exotic sinkwa, the balsam pear, the kiwano, and some even more mysterious fruits. And of course there are the squash and the pumpkin, which are so closely related that some don't make the distinction between them.

Ancient explorers, who didn't know any better, used to confuse these close relatives with the melon. Known for their exploitation and development of the Americas, these European adventurers named whatever new food products they found after what they already knew. So peppers were named after that other spicy plant, the Asian pepper. Potatoes were named after truffles — just another underground tuber to them — and yellow tomatoes were called after the apple *pomodoro*, or golden apple. Melons did not grow in the Americas, just as pumpkins and squashes did not grow in Europe. *Pompions* some called them, after the French *pompon*, a word of unknown origin that seems to express roundness by its sound alone.

Others say its name is derived from the Latin *pepo*, meaning 'melon,' itself derived from the Greek word for cooking, for this was the type of melon you had to cook before eating.

This short history, emphasizing the American background of the pumpkin and squash, has puzzled many food connoisseurs. Didn't the Roman Apicius, held to be the author of the first cookbook, have pumpkin recipes? Didn't Pliny, Martial, and other ancients mention it? And from the famous table conversations of Athenaeus, I can quote: "A pumpkin is not edible when raw, but is good to eat when boiled or baked," and he tells of a heated discussion, including Plato, about the species to which the pumpkin belonged. But close reading suggests that all these ancient references were actually citing different versions of what we would call gourds.

The gourd is a fruit from the eastern Mediterranean. Originally it came from India, according to the Romans. It's no wonder, then, that Spanish, Portuguese, French, and English travelers compared the American pumpkins with the melon. Today nobody will deny the pumpkin its American heritage, and even the gourd seems to have gained American citizenship. More than ever, food is internationalized, and we know no better way to express the family of man than through the family of its foodstuffs.

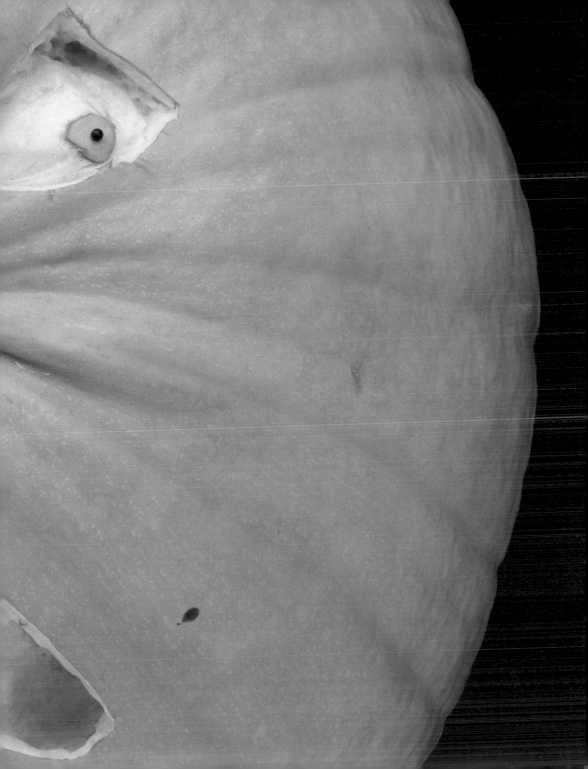

The Sacred and the Profane Pumpkin

Or, What Does It All Mean?

ook at a pumpkin and you know that it means business: it's big, it's round, and it's food, usually a lot of it. It's the whole world in a neat package, so what else can it mean? Just that: the world. And that is exactly what it meant in the Old World.

Because the "pumpkin" is a product of the New World, the Americas, you will not find any reference to it as such in the Old World. Its ancient name equivalent, however, was the gourd.

The New World considered the pumpkin one of the most important foodstuffs, together with corn (maize) and beans, all exclusive to the Americas, in which the pumpkin may have been the first cultivated food. The largest fruit of creation and full of seeds, it became a symbol of plenty.

In colonial America, food was a precious commodity and not something to be played with. As far as the importance of foodstuffs went, the prized pumpkin ranked high. However, with the arrival of other religions in the Americas, rites like the old Irish Oidhche Shamna, or the Vigil of Saman, provided an exception to the rule. On October 31st of each year, Saman, the lord of death, summoned his forces of darkness, and the population would burn fires to repel them. Thus was born the jack-o'-lantern — a carved pumpkin usually featuring a grinning face, baring a burning candle in its hollowed-out interior. Now a steadfast American tradition, jack-o'-lanterns appear in windows and on doorsteps every year at Halloween.

A puritan from New England is called a pumpkinhead because he sticks to old customs, and maybe that's why a pumpkinhead is also a blockhead, or a fool — someone with nothing but pulp between the ears. In China, where the gourd is as old as the world, it has a similar connotation. *Li T'ieh-kuai,* a double gourd or pumpkin that is shaped like an hourglass, is the second of the Chinese emblems representing the Eight immortals. It symbolizes the link between two opposites, like the upper and the lower world, day and night, or sorrow and joy. As a mythical figure, *Li T'ieh-kuai* was a man who could leave his body and visit the upper world, or heaven. This same symbol is not exclusively Asian but also present in the Western World, in an alchemical representation in which two pumpkins have the shape of two vases or amphorae. In both representations, the communication between the two containers is symbolized by a column of smoke.

Aficionados of the tarot can recognize this principle in Arcanum Nº 14, Temperance, in which an angel pours a white substance from a red vessel into a blue one — or vice versa. In Europe the pumpkin is usually associated with Cinderella, the girl who rode to the ball, where she met her prince charming,

in a pumpkin that had been turned into a
coach. At midnight the spell was broken
and the coach turned back into a large
pumpkin. Today we call it Pumpkin
Time when a lucky period, or a dream,
has come to an end, and we are once
more confronted with the harsh
realities of life.

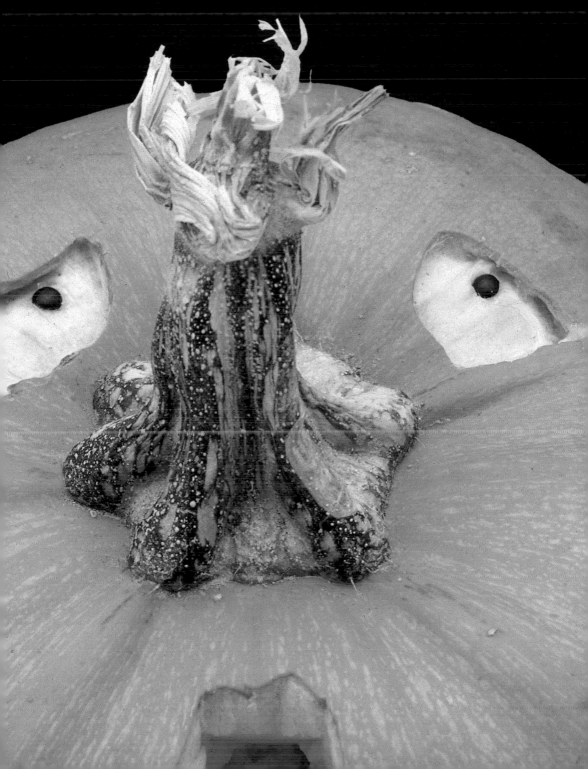

Grow Your Own Pumpkin

HE pumpkin is a vine with very heavy fruits. Under glass the plants will overpower the fruits as such; they will not be the giants you hope for until you transplant them outside. Still, pumpkin plants are best nurtured in the beginning under glass. Start by putting a couple of seeds in any type of container filled with good sowing compost and place under a glass cake cover or large glass bowl turned upside down, at the end of April. The seeds will germinate quite quickly at a temperature of 70 degrees Fahrenheit.

After a week you will begin to see the budding vines of your pumpkin plants. Now put the little plants (there should be two seedlobes) in separate medium-sized planters, until they grow to about five or six inches high. That way you can plant a decent, sturdy pumpkin outside in mid-May. Pumpkins require a lot of space, and the vines can easily reach five yards or more, so unless you are planning a pumpkin farm, one or a few plants will suffice.

Choose a spot in a corner, preferably near the compost heap. Pumpkin vines will help to get rid of any weeds, as they tend to suffocate them. If you do not have a convenient compost heap, make sure that area you choose contains enough nutrients in the soil. Now dig a hole and partially fill it with some rich compost. Next, cover the compost with a layer of ground soil and put your plants on top. The roots will find the treasure you have buried there, and the plants will prosper.

Usually it is not necessary to trim back the vines, but if another plant seems to suffer from a very expansive vine, just cut the excess off. Sturdy winter squashes and pumpkins will keep for a long time. Depending on the variety you choose, your autumn harvest may surprise you.

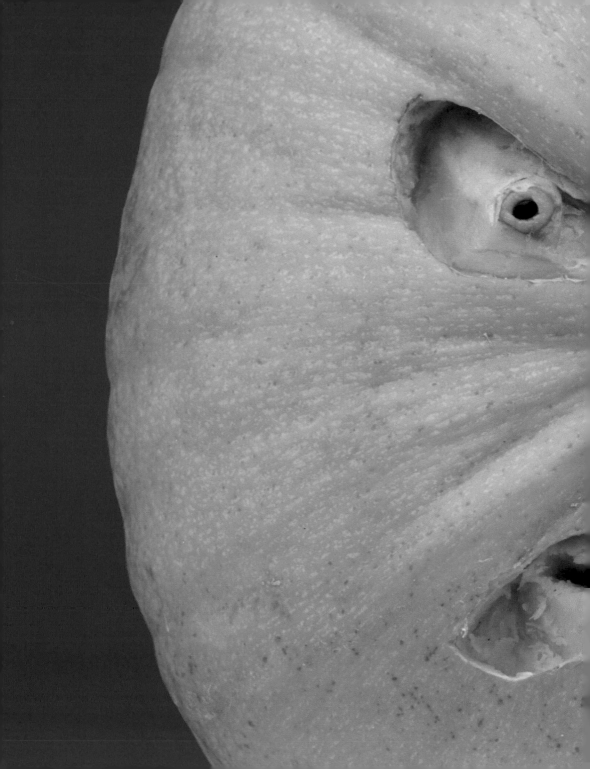

The Decorative Pumpkin

Or, the Nose Job

 UMPKINS are ideal guests for a come-as-you-are party. They do not need any extra work to decorate a table, a room, or an entire house.

No vegetable or fruit comes in so many colors, shapes, or sizes, and most pumpkins hardly need any preparation to be kept indefinitely. While they may seem to be too good to eat, some are better admired than eaten. Because a pumpkin or squash tend to wither like a flower, it is preferable to use ripe fruits with tough skins.

As color, shape, and size can vary so much, pumpkins can fit effortlessly into any interior. Buy a selection and put them on a plate, in a basket, or directly on a side table and enjoy this charming detail to your home.

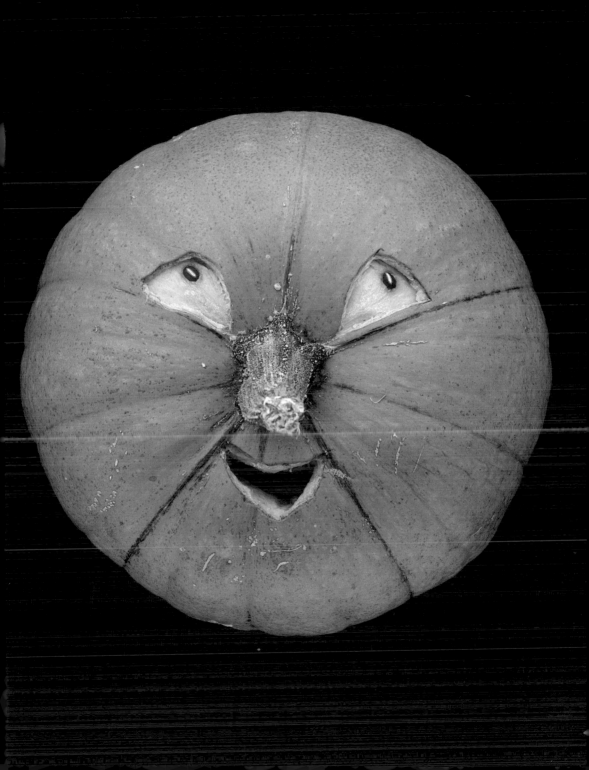

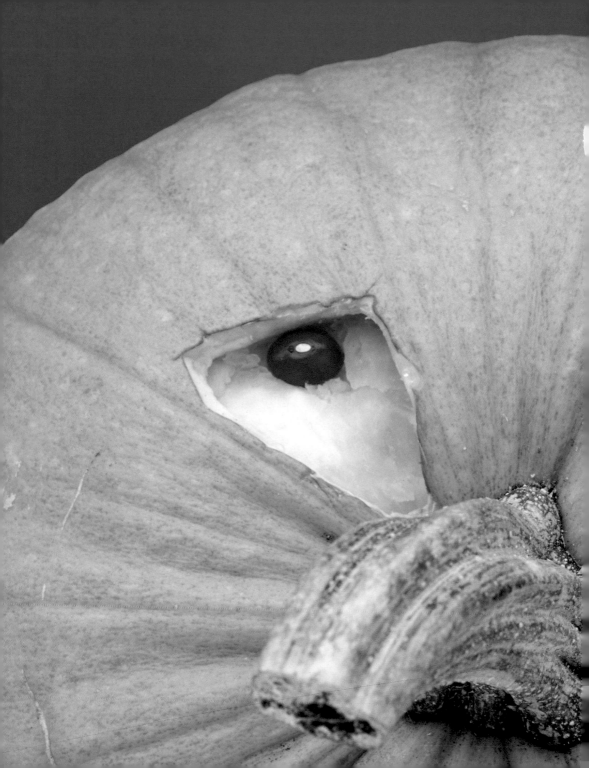

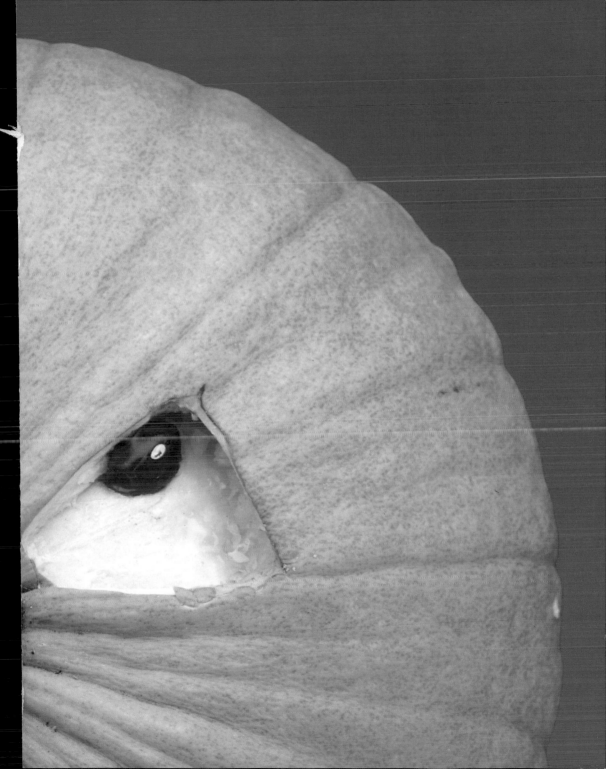

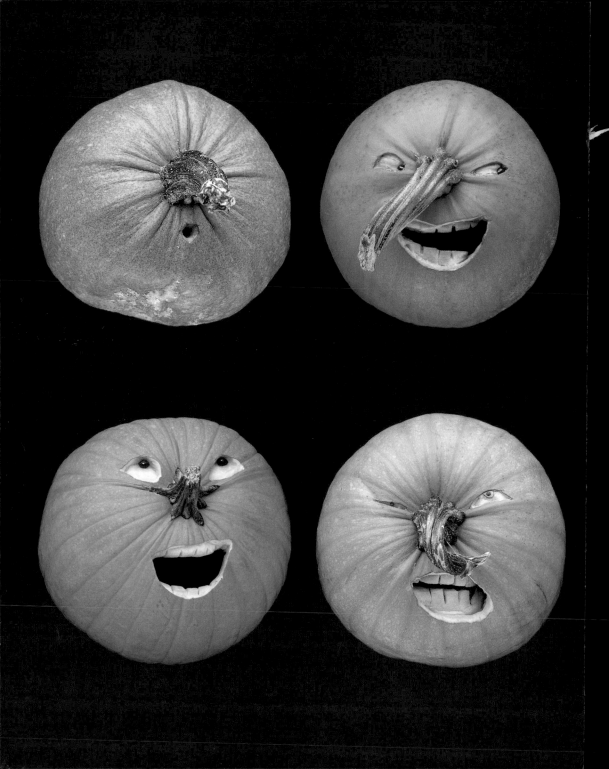

We could call the orange-colored giant the king of the pumpkin world. Its sturdy size, distinctive shape, and strong color give it an imposing presence. So some call it a pity that we deem it necessary to carve holes into the emperor of fruits to make it "function" as a lantern. Doesn't it shine enough on its own?

The traditional jack-o'-lantern is, well, traditional. We cut around the stem, hollow it out, cut out facial features, and put the lid on, with the stem featured as a kind of strange hairdo or hat. But let a designer look at a pumpkin, and he will give you a whole new way of looking at it.

The mouth is a hole, so designing a pumpkin mouth doesn't require a lot of effort. Eyes are sorts of holes: that too is pretty easy. But what about the nose? The nose is not a hole and a hole is no nose. It is just an indication that there should be something there.

You don't make a snowman's nose by putting a hole in his face. Rather, you use a carrot or a piece of coal, because it adds personality. The head has one major protrusion, the nose. The pumpkin has just one protrusion — its stem. Why not turn the stem into the nose of the jack-o'-lantern? That is the quintessential nose job. It was just too obvious to think of.

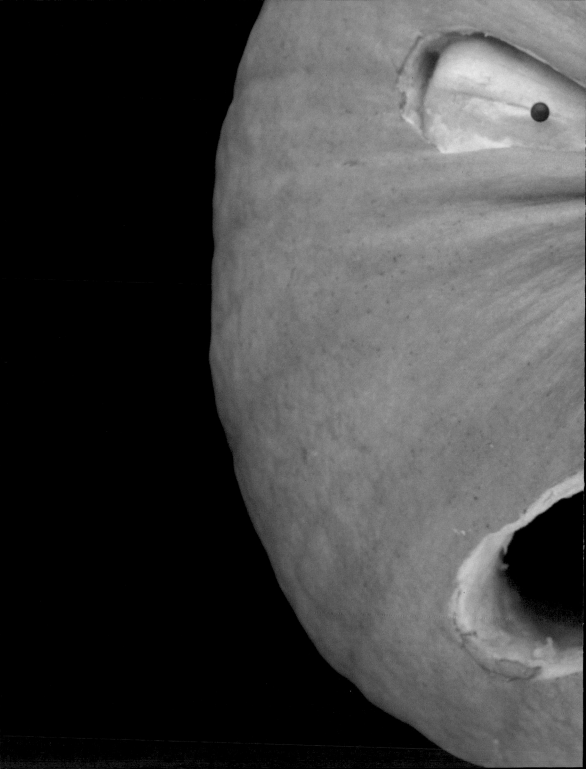

The Pumpkin as Gastronomic Delight All Over the World

s a New World food, the pumpkin has prospered everywhere, just like the potato and the tomato. Practically every country and its cuisine has a unique way of preparing it, from simpler cooking methods like baking, frying, or roasting, to more complicated dishes. Prepared either sweet or savory, it works well with strong flavors like fresh herbs, flavorful cheese, or strong pepper, while it can also complement any fine dessert, with added fruits, nuts, or even flower essence. Beyond any doubt, the pumpkin's versatility has made it a popular vegetable with food cultures from around the world.

Sometimes entire meals have been based upon the same main ingredient, although featured differently in every course, like Louis xvi's famous potato dinner, but nothing could fulfill multiple courses as flawlessly as the pumpkin.

Begin with a pumpkin soup, such as Paul Bocuse's thick, creamy soup, served in its own shell, or one of the many Italian versions, with the addition of orange juice or fennel. Follow it up with a succulent pie from Elba, or with tortelli or gnocchi from Italy, or, as the Dutch seem to prefer, with crunchy croquettes.

As a main course, pumpkin offers a lot of variety. Take the South American *carbonada criolla:* somewhat similar to Bocuse's soup, this stew is presented in the pumpkin shell itself. Or try the Arab version, *mderbel*, which contains lamb as well.

The French excel in all kinds of sweet and savory tarts, including a gratin that the painter Toulouse-Lautrec fancied. While in Germany they prefer a pumpkin purée called *Kürbisbrei*.

As an accompaniment, pickled pumpkin, whether from India or Germany, goes with a variety of main courses as do pumpkin sauces.

But the sweetish taste of the pumpkin gives most inspiration to lots of desserts and sweets. In Burgundy the *flamusse* is a traditional kind of pudding; in Persia they make a kind of jam or chutney with it; and from Indonesia to the West Indies, pumpkin is candied. In Portugal, thin strands of a type of spaghetti squash are candied in a special way, as *doce de chila*: after the fleshy threads of the *abobóra*, as it is called, are pulled out of the squash, they are cooked in hot syrup, flavored with lemon peel, and then dried. They are used in pies, tarts, puddings, and especially in egg-rich flans, like *morgado* and *toucinho do ceu*.

Like the pumpkin itself, the recipes featured in this book reflect the world.

Soupe de Courge

This is Paul Bocuse's famous thick pumpkin soup, from France, served inside the pumpkin shell

Soupe de Courge

1 pumpkin
    of 6 1/2 to 9 lbs.

6 to 7 cups croutons

1 cup grated
    Gruyere cheese

salt and pepper to taste

3 quarts of light cream

Cut a lid from the top of the pumpkin by cutting around the stem.
Remove and discard the seeds and fibers, but be sure to leave behind all meat.
Place the croutons and the cheese in a few alternating layers (until you run out) in the pumpkin. Season with salt and pepper.
Add the cream and cover well with the "lid."
Bake the pumpkin for 2 hours in a 350°F oven.

To serve the pumpkin: remove the lid, stir the contents gently with a spoon until the pumpkin flesh and the other ingredients are transformed into a deliciously thick soup. Taste and add more salt and pepper, if necessary.

Minestra di zucca con lenticchie

Pumpkin and lentil soup, Italy

Clean the fennel by cutting away the stalks and remove any brown parts, but keep the feathery

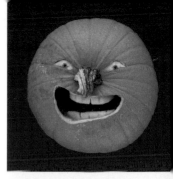

green leaves. Chop the bulb coarsely.
In a casserole sauté the onion in oil for about
10 minutes until golden. Then add the fennel,
and sauté for 5 more minutes. Add the lentils,
fennel seeds, water, and salt to taste and bring to
the boil. Simmer the ingredients for 30 minutes,
partly covered. Add the pumpkin or squash and
simmer for another 25 minutes, or until pumpkin
and lentils are done. Now add the chopped
fennel leaves just before serving and season with
salt and pepper.

Minestra di zucca
con lenticchie
1 small fennel bulb
4 tbs. extra-virgin olive oil
1 onion,
    coarsely chopped
1 cup rinsed lentils
1 tsp. fennel seeds
1 quart water
1/2 lb. raw pumpkin or
    butternut squash,
    diced
salt and pepper to taste

Stuffed Mini-Pumpkins

Stuffed mini-pumpkins make a refined garnish
for any roast, as well as duck, turkey, or game.
Start by first scooping out large balls of cooked
meat from a large pumpkin with a traditional
ice cream scooper. Next, hollow out the balls of
pumpkin meat with a smaller scoop, like a melon
baller. Purée any leftover pumpkin meat,
seasoning it any way you want, and then stuff the
balls with it.
For added fun you can garnish the tops of the
mini-pumpkins with cheese and then broil them
briefly before serving.

55

Gnocchi di zucca

Pumpkin gnocchi, Italy

Gnocchi di zucca

2 lbs., 3 oz. raw
   pumpkin meat

1 egg

2 tbs. olive oil

2 cups flour, sifted

salt and pepper

1/2 cup heavy cream

4 tbs. butter

12 basil leaves

freshly grated
   Parmesan cheese

Cut the pumpkin meat into chunks and steam until the pumpkin is very tender, about 10 to 15 minutes.

Purée the pumpkin in a food processor and then add the egg, oil, flour, salt, and pepper. Process until the mixture is smooth and does not stick. Shape the mixture into a roll ½ inch thick and then cut the roll into ½ inch slices. Next, place a fork, prong side up, on your work surface and sprinkle the area with flour. Now roll each ½ inch slice with a floured finger over the fork prongs, from tip to the handle.

Bring a pot of salted water to a boil and add the gnocchi.

Cook them until they are swollen and floating on the surface (approximately 2-3 minutes). In a separate saucepan, bring the cream to a gentle boil and add the butter. When the butter has melted, immediately pour the mixture into a bowl. Cut the basil finely with scissors directly over the bowl and mix.

Pour the sauce over the drained gnocchi and serve with freshly grated Parmesan cheese.

Tortelli di zucca

Pasta stuffed with pumpkin, Italy

Prepare the pasta by heaping the flour on a flat
surface and then make a well in the center of it.
Next add the salt and eggs to the well and
gradually mix the flour into the eggs from the
sides. Knead the resulting dough for 5 minutes;
let rest for at least 30 minutes wrapped in plastic
wrap. Then knead again for 3 minutes and let
it rest.

Purée the pumpkin meat (cooked on a greased
sheet in the oven at 350°F until tender, about
45 minutes) in a food processor and put into
a bowl.

Add the crumbled amaretti, the mostarda
di Cremona with a spoon of its juice, nutmeg,
sugar, salt, pepper, half of the Parmesan, bread
crumbs, and grappa, and mix thoroughly.

Roll out the pasta dough as thin as possible,
(about 1/16 inch) on a floured surface. Cut it into
3 ¼-inch-wide strips and cover the ones you
aren't working with.

Place teaspoons of filling about 1 ¾ inches apart
in a straight row, 2 ½ inches from the edge
of the sheet. Fold the edges of the strip over the
mounds of filling and press gently between each

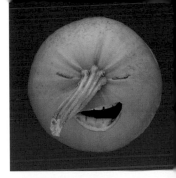

Tortelli di Zucca

homemade pasta
  (made with 2 3/4 cup
  flour, 3 eggs, and
  a pinch of salt)
1 pumpkin (2 lbs., 2 oz.)
1/2 cup Amaretti cookies,
  finely crumbled
2 oz. mostarda
  di Cremona
  (chutney, a specialty
  from Cremona,
  available from specialty
  shops), finely chopped
1/2 tsp. grated nutmeg
1/2 tsp. sugar
salt and freshly ground
  pepper
1 cup Parmesan cheese,
  freshly grated
1 tbs. dried bread crumbs
1 tbs. grappa
5 tbs. butter

mound. Next, cut between each mound using a pastry wheel, so you will get square stuffed pillows. Press the edges together, moistening them with a little cold water if necessary. Drop the tortelli carefully into a large pot of salted boiling water to which you have added a splash of olive oil and cook until done (about 5 minutes, depending on thickness of the dough) Melt the butter and pour it into a serving bowl. As soon as the tortelli are ready, let them drain a little and then put them in the bowl with the butter. Add the rest of the grated Parmesan cheese and serve immediately. Be sure to bring a chunk of Parmesan and a grater to the table for those guests who like extra cheese.

Dutch Pumpkin Croquettes

Cook the squash by first cutting it in half and putting it, cut sides down, on a greased baking sheet. Bake in a 350°F oven until almost done (about 45 minutes).
Scoop out the meat and purée it in a food processor. Mix the purée with the butter and egg yolks and then pepper, salt, and sugar to taste. Heat the purée in a pan, stirring constantly until

it thickens, taking care that it does not burn.
Pour onto an baking sheet and let cool and
set further.

Flour a tabletop and your hands and roll the
mass into small patties or croquettes about 1 inch
thick and 2 inches in diameter. Put in a cool
place to become firm (about 2 hours) then dip
them first into the beaten eggs and then in
the bread crumbs.

Deep-fry the croquettes at 350°F for about
4 minutes, or until golden brown, and serve
immediately.

A delicious accompaniment with game or fowl,
but also a nice snack.

Roast Pumpkin

Nothing is easier than roasting a pumpkin.
Pumpkin can be roasted with a piece of meat
(beef, veal, pork).

Cut slices of pumpkin into 1 ½ inch chunks,
leaving the skin in place to hold the pumpkin
together.

Cut away the seeds and fibers. Season the pieces,
and either arrange them in the fat around
the roast, or cook them in oil in a separate pan

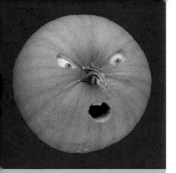

next to the roast. Tough pumpkin needs about an hour at 375°F, the normal roasting temperature. With beef, which needs a faster oven, 45 minutes should be enough.

Turn the pieces over occasionally.

Fried Pumpkin

Frying pumpkins is easy and delicious. Just cut slices from a whole pumpkin, remove the skin and the seeds, and dip the slices in flour that you have seasoned with salt and pepper.

Pan-fry them very delicately in butter until they are golden brown.

A Russian version is as follows:

Peel and slice the pumpkin and fry in butter. Remove the fried pumpkin slices and set aside. Fry ½ tablespoon of flour in ½ tablespoon butter, add 1 cup sour cream, and bring to boil. Pour the sauce over the pumpkin and serve.

Greek Pumpkin Fritters

Add the ingredients to a mixing bowl, in the order listed above, and mix well. If the mixture

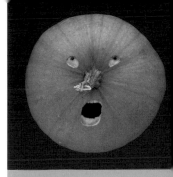

is too thick, add more water. Beat well.
Cut the pumpkin in ½ inch slices and remove
skin and seeds. Dip the slices into the batter
and shallow-fry them in a pan with ½ inch
of olive oil.

Carbonada Criolla

Rich stew in a pumpkin, Argentina

To prepare the pumpkin:
Cut a lid from the top but don't remove the
stalk. Discard the fibers and seeds and scoop
away the solid flesh, leaving a sturdy wall
of pumpkin, being careful not to pierce it.
Measure out 2 lbs. of the pumpkin flesh for
the stew.
Brush the inside with melted butter and sprinkle
lightly with sugar.
Replace the lid and set the pumpkin aside on
a baking sheet.
Cook the onion and garlic in a little oil until
soft, but not browned.
Transfer to a large saucepan.
Brown the beef in the oil and add it to the
onion mixture in the saucepan.
Add the tomatoes, tomato paste, half the stock,

*Carbonada Criolla
(continued)*
3 lbs. chuck steak, cubed
1 lb. tomatoes, peeled
  and chopped
1 tablespoon tomato
  paste
3 ½ pints beef stock
bouquet garni
1 heaping tsp. dried
  oregano
salt and pepper
2 lbs. sweet potatoes,
  peeled and cubed
2 lbs. potatoes,
  peeled and cubed
2 lbs. pumpkin,
  cut in chunks
2 cans sweet corn
12 canned yellow
  peach halves, sliced
syrup from
  canned peaches

61

Mderbel

1 lb., 2 oz. lamb,
   in 5 chunks

1 leek, cut in 5 pieces

2 tsp. salt

1 tsp. ground ginger

1 tsp. saffron powder

water

2 cups olive oil

1 lb., 2 oz. peeled
   pumpkin, cut into
   thin slices

2 tsp. ground cinnamon

2 tbs. sugar

the bouquet garni, a little salt and plenty
of pepper to the meat and onions.
Cover and simmer until the meat is almost
cooked (approximately 1 hour).
At this time, put the pumpkin shell in the oven
at 375°F. Leave it for 30 minutes, or longer if
the walls are thick. But be careful not to collapse
the walls! You can use a large casserole as
a support for the walls.
Add the sweet potato, potato, and pumpkin to
the saucepan and cover with more stock. Return
to a boil and simmer for 20-30 minutes, or until
the meat is tender, the potatoes are cooked,
and the liquid is thickened with the dissolved
pumpkin.
Stir in the sweet corn and peaches and simmer
for another 15 minutes. Taste, correcting the
seasoning and adding a little of the peach syrup.
Remove the bouquet garni and discard.
Ladle the stew into the pumpkin and put back
into the oven for 10 to 15 minutes and serve.

Mderbel

Lamb stew with pumpkin, Middle East

In a saucepan, combine the lamb, leek, salt,
ginger, saffron powder, water to cover, and half
of the olive oil. Cover the saucepan and simmer
for about 2 hours, or until the meat is tender.
In a heavy pan or casserole, heat the remaining
olive oil. Sauté the pumpkin slices slowly for
45 minutes, until golden on both sides.
Purée the pumpkin, add cinnamon and sugar,
and mix well.
Spoon the lamb onto individual plates. Mix the
cooking liquid with the pumpkin purée, and
ladle the mixture over the lamb.

French Pumpkin Sauce

French Pumpkin Sauce

1 lb., 3 oz. pumpkin

1 small shallot

1 1/2 tbs. unsalted butter

1 tsp. curry powder

a pinch of salt

freshly ground pepper

1/2 cup white wine

1 tbs. white port wine
  (can be replaced with
  medium dry sherry)

1 cup vegetable stock

1/2 cup heavy cream

1 tbs. whipped cream

Cut open the pumpkin, discard seeds and fibers,
and peel and dice the meat. Chop the shallot
and sauté it in the butter until transparent;
then add the pumpkin. Next add curry powder,
salt, and pepper. Turn the heat down low, so the
curry does not burn.
Add the wine, the port, and the stock.
Reduce the liquid by half and stir in the heavy

63

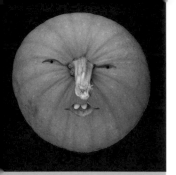

Kürbisbrei mit Äpfeln

2 lbs. diced pumpkin

2 oz. bacon

1 heaping tbs. butter

1 1/2 cup chopped onion

3/4 lb. apples

juice and rind of 1 lemon

salt and sugar

cream. Cook until the pumpkin is tender
(about 45 minutes). Purée and pass through
a sieve. Mix in the whipped cream just before
serving.

Kürbisbrei mit Äpfeln

Pumpkin and apple purée, Germany

Peel, seed, and cube the pumpkin.
Cut the bacon into pieces and fry them gently
in a large pan with butter. When the fat begins
to run from the bacon, add the onion, and allow
both to brown lightly to a golden color.
Add the pumpkin and about ¼ inch of water.
Cover closely and simmer for 10 to 15 minutes,
until the pumpkin begins to collapse.
Add the apples, peeled, cored, and cut into
chunks, a good squeeze of lemon juice,
and a teaspoon of grated lemon rind.
Season with a little salt and some sugar, just
enough to bring out the flavor. Continue to cook
uncovered at a low heat, so that the apple pieces
collapse and the juices evaporate. Pour off any
surplus liquid and correct the seasoning with
more lemon juice and salt, if necessary.

Gratin de Potiron

Toulouse-Lautrec's gratin of pumpkin, France

Peel the pumpkin, removing fibers and seeds.
Slice the wedges into pieces ¼ inch thick and
2 inches wide. Dip the pieces in the flour and
fry them in batches, one layer at a time, in the
oil until they are golden but not brown. Drain
well. In another pan cook the onions gently
in some oil until they are soft, but not colored.
Add the tomatoes, and raise the heat as their
juices begin to run. You should end up with
a moist mixture of onions bathed lightly
in tomato. Season with salt, pepper, and a little
sugar.

In a gratin dish, layer slices of pumpkin and the
onion mixture, adding a little extra seasoning.
Finish with a layer of pumpkin, then scatter the
gratin evenly with bread crumbs. Dribble melted
butter over the crumbs. Bake at 350°F for about
45 minutes, until the gratin is bubbling at the
sides. Finish browning the top under the broiler,
if desired.

Gratin de Potiron

2 lbs. pumpkin

flour mixed with a little
   salt and pepper

oil (as much as you need
   for shallow frying,
   depending on the size
   of the skillet)

1 lb. onions, diced

8 oz. tomatoes, peeled
   (or use canned ones)

salt and pepper

sugar

bread crumbs, as much
   as needed depending
   on the gratin dish

2 tbsp. butter or more,
   as needed for the
   gratin dish

Baked Pumpkin Purée

Boil pumpkin and potatoes together in salted water until soft.

Drain well and then mash into a purée.

Beat the eggs and stir them into the vegetables with 4 tablespoons of the butter.

Mix the cheeses together and add about half of the mixture to the purée.

Season according to taste, adding salt and plenty of black pepper and more cheese if needed.

Grease a gratin dish and pour the mixture into it. Sprinkle the top with the remaining cheese. Melt the last of the butter and dribble it over the top as evenly as possible. Bake at 350°F until nicely browned and the edges are bubbling.

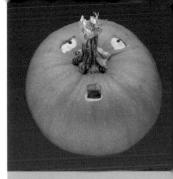

Torta di zucca

A hearty pumpkin pie, Italy

Halve and clean the squash or pumpkin and
cook it by baking it, cut sides down, on a greased
sheet in the oven at 350°F, for about 1 hour;
when tender, put the meat through a food mill
or potato ricer.

Melt the butter in a large skillet. Add the sage
and the garlic and sauté slightly, without letting
them color. Add the pumpkin, lower the heat,
and sauté for 15 minutes, stirring constantly.
Transfer to a bowl and let cool completely.
Remove the sage and the garlic from the bowl.
Preheat the oven to 375°F.

Heavily butter a 10-inch springform pan and line
it with bread crumbs.

Add the ricotta to the cold pumpkin. Stir until
completely smooth. Add Parmesan, eggs, salt and
pepper to taste, and a pinch of nutmeg, and mix
well. Transfer the mixture to the prepared pan
and bake for 70 minutes, until firm and golden
on top.

Let the torta rest on a rack for 15 minutes before
releasing the form.

Cut into slices and decorate with a few sage
leaves.

Torta di zucca

2 lbs. of butternut
squash or pumpkin

4 tbs. unsalted butter

4 large, fresh sage leaves

2 large cloves garlic,
peeled but left whole

2 cups ricotta, drained

1/2 cup freshly
grated Parmesan

4 extra-large eggs

salt and pepper

nutmeg

2 tbs. sweet butter

Tarte de Potiron

aux Pruneaux

7 oz. sweet pie crust

2 1/4 cup whole milk

1/2 vanilla bean

1 cinnamon stick

1 pumpkin (14 oz.), diced

1 cup raw cane sugar

1 stick (1/4 lb.) butter

1/2 cup crème fraîche

4 egg yolks

5 oz. prunes,
    pitted (3/4 cup)

Tarte de Potiron aux Pruneaux
Pumpkin pie with prunes, France

Line a pie pan with the pie crust, cover the crust
with foil, and weight down with the pits of the
prunes (or baking beans).
Bake for about 10 minutes.
Remove beans and foil.
Bring the milk to a boil. Add the vanilla bean
and the cinnamon stick for a couple of minutes
and then remove and discard them.
Add the diced pumpkin meat and ½ cup of sugar
to the saucepan. Cook for 15 minutes.
Add butter, crème fraîche, and egg yolks,
and purée.
Press the purée through a fine sieve to remove
the fibers of the pumpkin. Pour the mixture
into the pie crust, pressing the prunes into the
mixture. Sprinkle the top with the remaining
sugar. Bake for 30 minutes in a 400°F oven,
broiling the tarte briefly at the end to caramelize
the top. Serve warm.

Traditional American Pumpkin Pie

Line a 9-inch pie pan with the pastry and refrigerate.

In the meantime put pumpkin, sugar, spices and salt in a food processor or beat with a beater in a bowl. Then beat in milk, eggs, cream, and brandy. Pour into the unbaked pastry shell and bake in a preheated 325°F oven for 1 hour, or until a knife inserted in the center comes out dry. Cool. Serve with cheddar cheese or whipped cream mixed with crystallized ginger.

Traditional American
Pumpkin Pie
pastry for 1 pie crust
  (made with 2 cups
  plain flour, 1 tsp. salt,
  5 1/2 oz. shortening,
  5 to 6 tsp. ice water)
2 cups cooked pumpkin
2/3 cup brown sugar,
  firmly packed
2 tsp. cinnamon
1/2 tsp. ground ginger
1/2 tsp. salt
3/4 cup milk
2 eggs, well beaten
1 cup heavy cream
1/4 cup brandy

Flamusse

Burgundian pumpkin flan, France

Place the pumpkin cubes in a heavy pan with
2 tbs. of water, cover, and let simmer for
7-8 minutes.

Remove the lid and continue to cook, stirring
often, until the pumpkin flesh collapses into
a purée.

Drain and cool the pumpkin meat, forcing it
through a fine sieve.

In a bowl, beat the eggs, sugar, and salt until
the sugar dissolves and the mixture is white and
foamy. Fold in the sifted flour, a little at a time,
followed by the crème fraîche.

Preheat the oven to 350°F. Butter a large soufflé
dish or individual soufflé molds.

Melt the remaining butter, pour it into the egg
mixture followed by the purée.

Put the mixture into the dish or individual molds
and bake it for 30 minutes.

Slide a knife along the flan so it will free itself of
the mold when given a good shake. If it doesn't
loosen, put it back in the oven for a few minutes.

Süßsaurer Kürbis

Pumpkin pickles, Germany

Peel and slice the pumpkin. Discard seeds and
fibers. Cut the flesh in cubes and marinate them
overnight in a mixture of water and vinegar.
Bring sugar, water and vinegar mixture, ginger
and cloves to a boil. Add the drained pumpkin,
reduce the heat, and simmer until the pumpkin
is transparent.
Transfer with a slotted spoon into sterilized jars.
Reduce the liquid until it forms a nice syrup,
enough to cover the pumpkin. Store in a cool
place.

Kaddu ka Achaar

Pickled pumpkin, India

Wash and dry the pumpkin. Cut into long,
thin slices. Remove seeds and fibers, if any,
Parboil in water and drain. Let the pumpkin dry
in a cool place. Dry-roast the ingredients,
from cumin to salt, in a pan for 2 to 3 minutes.
Grind them together, add lemon juice, and make
a paste.
Brush the pumpkin slices with the paste and put

Kaddu ka Achaar

1 lb. green pumpkin

1 tsp. each of white
    cumin, carom (ajowan),
    coriander,
    and fenugreek seeds

1/4 tsp. turmeric powder

2 tbs. mango powder
    (amchoor)

8 black peppercorns

1 tsp. garam masala

sea salt to taste

2 tbs. lemon juice

1/2 cup mustard oil
    (pressed from mustard
    seed, an Indian product,
    available from specialty
    shops)

71

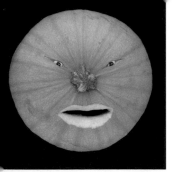

Bal Kabagi Tatlisi

2 lbs. pumpkin

2/3 cup sugar

2 tbs. water

2 cloves

1 cup walnuts, chopped

them in a clean, dry glass jar with a lid.
Heat the oil, let it cool, and pour it over the
pumpkin slices. Cover the jar and place it outside
or in the sun for 3 to 4 days (bring it in at night).
Shake at least once a day.
Carom can be replaced by thyme, if unavailable,
but most ingredients can be obtained in
Indian shops.

Bal Kabagi Tatlisi
Pumpkin dessert, Middle East

Cut the pumpkin into 1-inch cubes and place in
a shallow pan. Sprinkle with sugar, add the water
and cloves, and cover. Cook over very low heat
for about 30 minutes. Cool in the pan.
Place in a serving dish and garnish with the
walnuts.

Kolak Labu

Pumpkin in creamy coconut, Indonesia

Peel and clean the pumpkin. Dice the flesh and
boil in 2 cups of water for 5 minutes. Drain.
In another saucepan, simmer the santen with a
pinch of salt and the brown sugar, stirring often
and being careful that the santen does not quite
come to a boil. When the sugar is dissolved,
add the diced pumpkin and simmer, about 5 to
8 minutes, until cooked. Serve hot. Can be
prepared in advance, and reheated — carefully —
before serving.

Persian Pumpkin Jam

Put all the ingredients in a heavy saucepan and
heat gently until the sugar has dissolved.
Bring to a boil, then reduce the heat and cook
moderately for 25 to 30 minutes or until setting
point is reached. Pour into a warm, sterilized jar,
leave to cool, cover, and store.

Kolak Labu

1 lb. pumpkin

2 cups thick santen
    (coconut milk)

1/3 cup brown sugar

pinch of salt

2 cups water

Persian Pumpkin Jam

8 oz. finely grated
    pumpkin flesh,
    or pumpkin pulp
    (chopped in a food
    processor)

1 cup sugar

2 tbs. rosewater

finely grated rind and
    juice of 1 large lemon

1 tsp. ground cinnamon

73

Pumpkin Glossary

Varieties of Pumpkins, Squashes, and Gourds

Acorn: Acorn-shaped winter squash, 1 to 2 pounds and 4 to 8 inches
    long. The dark green skin is smooth and glossy, fluted and
    sometimes streaked with orange-yellow. The meat is orange.

Buttercup: A type of turban (winter) squash, with a bulbous cap.
    On top of the gray-flecked rind grows a pale gray head;
    diameter from 4 to 8 inches, weight 1 to 2 pounds. The meat
    is yellowish orange.

Butternut: Bright yellow winter squash with a round head and a long
    neck; 2 to 3 pounds and 8 to 12 inches long.

Calabaza: The generic Spanish name for squash, but also the name
    for some specific varieties that look like pumpkins with a whitish
    green skin.

Courgette: See Zucchini

Crowngourd: See Pattypan

Custard marrow: See Pattypan

Cymling: See Pattypan

Hubbard: A large winter squash, oval-shaped, and often very irregular. Size: 10 to 12 inches; weight 3 to 4 pounds. The skin is often dark green and may tend to run deep orange. The meat is orange-yellow.

Marrow: See Zucchini

(Marrow is the British name for squashlike vegetables.)

Patisson: See Pattypan

Pattypan: Another name for the custard marrow or crowngourd, cymling, or scalloped squash. This last name reveals something of its appearance: it is cream-colored when ripe, and flat with a scalloped circumference. The French call it *patisson*. Varieties include the White Bush, Peter Pan, and Custard Yellow. Size: 4 to 6 inches; weight ½ to 1 pound.

Pumpkin: Best known for its presence at Halloween and as Cinderella's coach, it is the archetypal winter squash, used in hundreds of recipes, not just pumpkin pie. It can measure from a mere few pounds to over 100 pounds, and its color, outside and inside, is usually dark orange, although it can run lighter in color to white. *Pumpkinification*, the act of turning into a pumpkin, is an old concept; even the ancient Greeks had a special word for it. Size: from small (7 inches, 10 pounds or even smaller) to huge, like the Big Max (20 inches, 100 pounds).

Scalloped squash: See Pattypan

Spaghetti: A winter squash, like an elongated melon with a yellow skin. Its name is derived from the spaghettilike strands in which the meat divides itself after cooking. (Cook it whole, cut it in half,

scoop out the seeds, and then scrape out the spaghettilike meat
with a fork). The structure makes it possible to leave the meat
slightly crunchy. Size: 10 inches; weight 4 to 7 pounds.

Sugar pumpkins: Sweet, small globe-shaped and ridged pumpkins,
orange on the outside and the inside. Size: 6 to 7 inches;
weight 7 to 8 pounds.

Turban: Almost a family by itself, in different sizes and color
combinations, but all with a wide, doughnut-shaped base, crowned
with a dome-shaped top. It looks almost too good to eat (many use
them just for decoration), but the orange-yellow meat is delicious.
Size: up to 15 inches; weight 7 to 8 pounds.

Wax gourd: Large, egg-shaped-to-elongated gourd with a greenish tint
hidden beneath a layer of whitish wax. The meat is white.
The half-ripe fruits are eaten. Ripe, the meat is not eaten, but the
rind is dried and used as a container, from small to fairly large.

White gourd: See Wax gourd

Yellow crookneck: A yellow straightneck with a crooked neck.

Yellow straightneck: Looks like a small baseball bat with a sturdy yellow
skin and soft yellow meat that both toughen and discolor with age.
The young ones, under 6 inches or 1 pound, are best.

Zucchini: A summer squash, also called courgette. There are several
varieties: dark green, light green, striped or flecked, and even
yellow. They are shaped like a cucumber; when ripe they are fatter,
like an eggplant, but they are best when young and small.

Pumpkin Tips

Pumpkin meat can still contain long, tough strings, even after those in the core have been removed. Use an electric beater to mash cooked pumpkin meat: the strings will wind around the beaters and can easily be removed.

If you want to prepare a pumpkin well in advance for Halloween, spray a little rubbing alcohol or antiseptic inside and outside to kill any the germs that may live there. Your pumpkin will stay fresh much longer. *But* be sure to keep away any fire until the fluids have evaporated!

When making a thick pumpkin soup or sauce, let the cooked pumpkin drain thoroughly before proceeding; the cooking liquid will spoil the taste of the cooked pumpkin meat. With gratins it is even more essential as the cooking liquid will drown your dish.

The best way to treat any pumpkin or squash is not to boil it,
but to grill, bake, or steam it. Boiling tends to dilute the taste.
The most practical way to cook it is to cut it in half and put it cut
side down on a slightly greased baking sheet. Bake it in the oven
until tender. (Depending on size, from 30 to 90 minutes at 350°F.)
Let it cool a while, then turn over the halves and scoop out the
fibers and seeds. Now you can prepare the tender meat any way
you like, like cutting the halves in large slices and grilling them,
or scooping out the meat and making a purée.

To make an ideal soup tureen out of a pumpkin, cut around the
stalk at the top, which will make a lid with a handle. Scrape the
seeds and fibers from the center with a spoon and replace with
croutons, grated cheese, and cream and put it in the oven for
two hours or more, depending on the size, at 350°F. Or you can
scrape out the meat from the inside, make a soup, and pour
it into the pumpkin.

**Do not throw away the seeds you have scraped from the inside
of the pumpkin.** Clean them by rinsing them and removing
the strings and dry them. Hulled and salted, the seeds make
a healthy and nourishing snack: spread on newspaper in one layer
and leave them to dry for at least 6 hours. Hull them and then
toss the seeds with a little vegetable (canola) oil and spread them
on a baking sheet.
Bake in a moderate oven (350°F) until they are golden brown

(30 minutes), stirring them every 5 to 10 minutes to toast them evenly. Salt and pepper to taste, let cool, and keep in closed jars.

Pumpkins and winter squashes can often be too hard to cut. However their soft spot is where the stem is. First cut off the stem, then pierce the pumpkin there and start cutting down the side.

To make cutting easier, prick the skin of the pumpkin in a few places and then heat it on high for 1 to 2 minutes in the microwave. (Piercing the skin first in a few places, prevents the pumpkin or any other vegetable from bursting or even exploding.)